Anne Caldwell

NEITHER HERE NOR THERE

SV

SurVision Books

First published in 2024 by
SurVision Books
Dublin, Ireland
Reggio di Calabria, Italy
www.survisionmagazine.com

Copyright © Anne Caldwell, 2024

Cover image: "Fabric Reflection" by Dave Bowie Jr.
© Dave Bowie Jr., 2024

Design © SurVision Books, 2024

ISBN: 978-1-912963-47-8

This book is in copyright. No part of this publication may be reproduced, stored in a retrieval system, or transmitted in any form or by any means without the prior permission in writing from the publisher.

Acknowledgements

Grateful acknowledgement is made to the editors of the following, in which some of these poems, or versions of them, originally appeared:

100 Words of Solitude, global voices in Lockdown 2020 (ed. by Simon Holloway, Philippa Holloway, Rare Swan Press, Switzerland, 2020): "Blue"

Alcatraz: a Poetry Anthology (ed. by Cassandra Atherton, Paul Hetherington, Gazebo Books, 2023): "Aqueduct"

Dreaming Awake: New and Contemporary Prose Poetry from the United States, Australia and the United Kingdom (ed. by Cassandra Atherton and Peter Johnson, MadHat Press, 2023): "Live Streaming Friday," "Dancing Slippers," and "The Roost"

Metamorphic: 21 Century Poets respond to Ovid (ed. by Nessa O'Mahony, Paul Munden, Recent Work Press 2017): "Fallen"

Spelt Magazine: "Desire Path"

Tract: Prose Poems (ed. by Paul Munden, Monica Carroll, *Recent Work Press, 2017):* "Glass Blower"

"Philomela" won the first prize in the Frodsham Literature Festival competition 2023.

In *The Shut Drawer*, the quote is from *The Grassling* by Elizabeth Jane Burnett.

This collection is dedicated to Dave Bowie Jr.

CONTENTS

Aqueduct	7
Fallen	8
Glass Blower	9
Now	10
Blue	11
The Applecart	12
Desire Path	13
Philomela	14
Hygge	15
A Step at a Time	16
Late Snow	17
Red Tulips	18
Live Streaming Friday	21
Safe Passage	22
Seabed	23
Love Poem	24
Slippage	25
Puppet Speak	26
Not I	28
Dancing Slippers	29
The Shut Drawer	30
The Roost	31

Among the Danes, lapwings are said to be the souls of women who died unmarried, while green sandpipers are the souls of old bachelors.

Christopher Morema, *On the Relationships between Birds and the Spirits*

Aqueduct

Walls were less rigid when I was young. Bedrooms expanded when love bloomed and contracted as grief swallowed the family, made it lemon-sour and pithy. Hiding in the bottom of the wardrobe, I would listen to the bitterness of mother and father. I'd a penknife, a lucky stone and a ball of string. I owned a hand-me-down bike and found a cycle route to Astbury, cutting beneath the canal aqueduct. The air was damp and cool; the brickwork smothered in moss.

A stalactite childhood lay here, lingering beneath that body of water. Beneath tadpoles and crested newts; beneath rusty shopping trollies and lead fishing sinkers.

Fallen

And when the wax melted I slammed into the water, remembering all those who tried before me: who'd leapt from mountain and cliffs, towers and columns. Those whose belief in the impossible was secure, those of us who have longed to soar with birds, ride thermals with ease, know how to catch the earth's slipstreams.

I watched cirrus clouds touched with gold as the sun sank beneath the Mediterranean waves. Felt my blood darken like lost hope, pooling at the back of my skull. I thought of my father. He was one of life's dreamers, one of Larkin's lecturers, lispers, Losels, loblolly-men.

Overhead, starlings swooped and curved across the sky. They were mocking me. A jumble of feathers, broken tibia and fibula. Father's daughter. My fingers burnt.

Glass Blower

And this dim-lit life is a glass vase in the making. Needs blowing and warming. Alice loads her rod with molten liquid from the furnace, rolling the orange glow to over 900 degrees in wet newspaper. Life begins to cool a little and harden. She doesn't wear gloves as she dips the glass in powdered cobalt. She blows, then places her thumb over the rod until the glass begins to swell into a sphere, catching an air bubble at its centre. Keep turning. Keep blowing. Find life's heat and joy. Don't stop moving.

Now

> *let this chill be moved from me.*
> *let it be now, let it be now.*
> —Helen Ivory, *Kite*

Now is so difficult to hold to, slippery as line-caught mackerel. Easier to gorge on yesterday's soda bread or the crescent-shaped biscuits of tomorrow.

Now is a copper saucepan, coated with olive oil, garlic just about to burn.

Now slips away like a driftwood-smile, or a stroll to the seashore, a pebble-washed Sunday or a Spring moon waxing and waning.

Now is the well-seasoned risotto or a pause in late night, milky conversations.

A train pulling into that country station where no one climbs aboard and no one leaves, and the poem's already full of bird song, well-written.

Blue

For now, we're marooned and separate: self-isolating in the face of what might come. My son's gloomy as a gunboat ferrying up and down the channel of his life so far. His navigation's unclear and circumstances take an unexpected turn, cutting across the rapids. Yet, here on the moors the curlews have returned: they're nesting in the field above Top Brink. I walked the hills at dusk last night and heard them bubbling and murmuring to each other, like water rising from a spring. For days the sky is Yves Klein blue. No planes, just endless crows circling overhead.

The Applecart

Loneliness is a Ford Fiesta, up on cinderblocks. I have kissed 22 people and can hear them all, shifting like moles through the warm soil. If I could touch you, darling, it would be a small miracle, a splash of water from Lourdes on the fingertips. If you could smell me, I'd be wild and unkempt, sweet as Cox's Orange Pippins ripening in the woodshed. I'd taste of yellow silk, rustling against the tongue. Our Manchester days are long forgotten. The library is a dome to silence, books sleeping in the storeroom. Loneliness is a Mustang with its engine roaring. All the walkers and ramblers are giving me a wide berth. I know they have to, but we're all toppling into the ginnel and snickets of despair like dominoes. Even Margaret. She died three years ago. 'It's right gradley today,' I remember her calling like a wild cat stuck in a cellar. Then again, she only had one lung. This evening, the moles are gathering in underground chambers, feasting on sherry and tarte tatin. Upturning the applecart. I want to fly across the rooftops, like Chagall's green goat and gather up the planets. A celestial apple harvest. *Il mondo è impazzito.* The world is spinning out of reach.

Desire Path

I dream of trees with blunt fingers and stars with sharp edges. An emerald city growing larger every time I close my eyes. The skyline shimmers in the distance, just out of reach. Above the rooftops the sky is hazy and stormy, heavier than normal as if all the woes of the world are pressing down.

Single men and women are cocooned behind closed doors, gazing out at a blue moon through blinds, curtains, plate glass, smokescreens, triple-glazing and high perimeter fences. I think of the desire path that cuts from cathedral to train station, past the fountain and a precious stretch of green. The dirt route crosses the garden of a music academy, skirting the medieval library with oak tables and manuscripts chained to shelves. I remember holding hands. The touch of him, skin to skin, the whorls of his fingertips, palms roughened by years in the theatre workshop, sanding and planing. And the city trees with their blunt fingers seem to be waving. I'm sure they are waving, not drowning.

Philomela

When he licked his lips and clambered on top of me in that dirty hut I stared at the sky through a gap in the roof. I watched the cloud-patterns, pictured marble fountains, hidden courtyards, the clean mosaics of Athens. I made myself blank, like folded linen. Cursed his name until the air was bluer than the sea. Cursed his life of wine. Candied fruit had rotted his teeth to blackened stumps. His breath was rank, an old dog scavenging for offal on the kitchen floor.

His belly pressed me flat, squashed my ribcage as I tried to shout. I scratched myself until I bled, then bit his ear. He whipped his knife out from his belt, grabbed me by the hair; forced my mouth wide open with his fist. *Stick your tongue out, girl.* That's all I remember. There it was, quivering at my feet, like an adder that had been cut in two and would not rest. How I longed for speech! To feel words forming, rolling around my mouth like sugared dates.

My sister and I cut up his son and served him to his father. Chopped tomato, bay leaf, pounded cinnamon and nutmeg; brought the *stifado* to the boil, simmered flesh until the sauce thickened. The boy was tender, spiced with all that anger. Now the three of us are avian: a swallow, a hoopoe, and me a nightingale. Our bones are hollow with grief or spite, our feathers tinged with blood. In the evening, you'll hear me singing. I've the sweetest voice.

Hygge

Webbed feet ran in the family, along with the ability to punctuate. We considered ourselves blessed, with our firm grasp on syntax even though the world outside was a blur of mud and quicksand. My father was a lock keeper, adept at catching eels. Our house never quite dried out, and we lived our subterranean lives deep within the Fens. My sentences were sluice gates and metaphors were watery. Father said that language was a slippery beast by nature and he would know; for he rarely wore shoes and liked the feel of the Ouse between his frog-like toes. The day the sea flooded our home, we scrambled up to the second floor, shivering. Father cut a hole in the plaster ceiling with a breadknife and we yearned for safe passage to higher ground.

Hygge: to comfort or console (Danish).

A Step at a Time

The deep-water channels of Fosdyke and King's Lynn make their leisurely way towards the North Sea. In no hurry. Here are the places where a few eels still thrive. They're dreaming of the ocean, the *Wide Sargasso Sea*, where they drifted in their tiny glass state, instinct calling them back to the Fens. I used to picture them lurking in the dark as I caught the cross-country train into Norfolk: Water Orton, Nuneaton, Narborough, Stamford, March, Ely. A slow train indeed. A thin strip of land beneath big skies, reed beds and potato fields.

Today, I think of you heading out into the city once more. You'll visit an exhibition, see Warhol's love of colour and line and the Thames beneath you, murky but beautiful. The Firth of Forth and the River Esk will be calling, playing their melodies somewhere in your heart.

Late Snow

My dead brother stood between us when we kissed. He took to lying with us at night: a shallow impression on the sheets, I felt him. He was the ghostly albatross around our necks, a devil on our shoulders. Even when having sex, we sensed we were being watched. You grew irritable and moody. For a while, Love was a ship marooned in ice. You spent days in pyjamas refusing to leave the house. I could hear you at night, opening the fridge, working your way through blocks of cheese and packets of Jacobs cream crackers, staring out of the window at the passage of Venus. *Three's a crowd,* you muttered. I was the one who went for supplies and bought you cigarettes whilst my brother flexed his impossible wings.

That spring, snow came late and three lambs died of hypothermia in the lower field. The farmer slung them over his shoulder and carried their stiff bodies to his trailer. The ewes bleated for days, nosing their way beneath holly bushes, trying to find their offspring's scent. The snow melted and Hope became a *thing with feathers*. Without a second glance, my brother was gone. Crocuses bloomed in the yard and our open door was a cautious smile.

Red Tulips

I.

Grief is a pokey office at the college with a view across Bolton town centre. Saddleworth Moor in the distance. The light forever rain-soaked, the sky mute; cumulus nimbus towering on the horizon. Dust gathers in the corners of the room. A tutorial list flaps on a drawing pin in the corridor and the world has gone virtual.

    I turn at the sound of my diary dropping on the Lino. Its pages are blank. There's a photograph of Hamish in his hand-knitted hat, just behind my shoulder, staring at the camera. He's holding a box made from science lab school furniture. *I've had my espresso, I'm heading out for a short walk across the fields now,* he texts. It took him weeks and weeks of sanding to get the plywood box so beautiful to touch.

II.

I make a list for the day ahead: duster, cleaning stuff, roller, white spirit. In the stillness, I close my eyes and listen to an army of delivery vans driving past the front window. Wind in the chimney. Hamish's box has no sharp edges and smells of damp cat, firelighters, ash cooling in the grate. I stroke the wood and remember my mother's rocking chair, arms worn smooth by forty years of her palms against the grain and curve of oak. The box opens and grief spills across the cork tiles.

    Behind me, there's a painting of four red tulips against an emerald background. Karen painted it for my wedding. She wrote *To Anne and Lee – Green Rubies – Love you* on the mounting board. I've been divorced for ten years now. I step into the picture, the fridge humming quietly to itself. I see my diary and stoop to pick it up, but it is as heavy as a sofa.

III.

I close my eyes and there's the contents of Auntie Margaret's flat on the pavement. A fridge, a wooden bookcase, standard lamp, magazine rack, electric fire and four good dining-room chairs with leatherette seat pads. I'm next of kin. The executer. Her death certificate says *extreme frailty. Covid complications.* All I can hear is the sound of jackdaws squabbling in the chimney. I imagine their shock of feathers. Pete next door is standing in his porch, trying to get my attention. His voice is muffled beneath his mask: a mournful bass note to the day.

Live Streaming Friday

Hours and hours of pish and mizzle up here on the moor's rim. I'm soaked to the skin. Yet again. My sunflowers hang their yellow petticoats towards the clarty earth, yet runner beans are blooming, jewelling hazel poles, stems entwined like lovers. Soon the afternoon will clear, free as a doodle, humming with solitary bees, hoverflies, ladybirds, lacewings. I've my headphones on, listening to the way your bass strolls deeply into the landscape of a song, letting all other instruments feel for their roots. There's an effortless shimmy, a saunter, a skedaddle to the way you play in conversation with your best mate's bright, alto sax. Today melody is a sparrowhawk, gliding above the heather.

Safe Passage

The Brazilian ornithologist Augusto Ruschi's stowed his birds in a suitcase to transport them on plane flights by lowering their temperature and placing them in torpor.

I carried the hummingbirds across the Atlantic on a flight that crossed time zones, the Mid-Atlantic rift and all the grief-stained chambers of my heart. The hummingbirds snoozed in their pyjamas like swaddled infants. I remember the moment when I warmed them and released them. They flew into the bright blue skies of Costa Rica. I too have been in some strange torpor for a year.

And now I have you. A flowering. An opening. A flowering again.

On Sunday we heard a Flamenco guitar after two years of silence and now there's a stretching of wings, a humming in my mind, an urge for duende. Later I will serenade the sheep in the Crimsworth fields. The spikey teasels are still flowering in the hedgerows of Yorkshire as the season turns.

Seabed

As your world is black and white, you become the pilot on the Nautilus. Beyond the razor-dazzle of sunlight. Here, you find your tribe: amongst the tube worms, mussels and shrimp. You discover cities of deep-sea coral where the dead rest their weary heads. Down in the abyssal zone, your life is chemical and pure. You discover delight in the 50 shipwrecks lying on the ocean floor with all their amphora and clinker-planks intact. You're saddened by the mountains of plastic in the Mariana Trench but here is bioluminescence and hydrothermal wonder. Down here, your silence is a draft of cold Guinness, soothing a heart parched of tenderness or love.

Love Poem

Your words are bats at night, hanging in the trees, waiting for midges to gather, stringing themselves out in convoluted clauses, swooping through the warm evenings, sometimes coalescing into jottings, loose collections, snippets of half heard conversations. Your words are musical and delicate. They're cave dwellers, preferring coolness to heat, the dripping of water over stone, the slow spreading of moss and lichen, the heart's inner chambers.

Your words roost for a while and fall head over heels when introduced to mine in late September. Unexpected juxtapositions delight them, and so begins our sonic chatter. Our words soar, zigzag through the night air above the winter jasmine.

Slippage

In a West Runton garden, beneath a pot used to force rhubarb, a family of fieldmice lie curled together, yearning for spring. The babies are fleshy and blind, like a jumble of ear lobes. They listen for crocus and narcissi nosing through the gravel. Ray is tending the moss-covered patio. He sleeps in a camper van parked at the end of the lane, with a cat curled on the driver's seat. This may be a rumour. Later, I watch him slowly digging in mulch and re-planting hydrangea. He's a man of few words.

On the foreshore, chalk
yields up a treasure trove:
bi-valves and corals.

Ray talks of a landslip down on the sea-cliffs. It's the longest he's ever spoken and the words roll around his mouth like new potatoes. He tells me the fossil of a mammoth is looming out of the mud, tusks first. A jumble of vertebrae and thighbones, tibia and fibula. The largest ever found in England. I picture the creature, buried in sand-strata, waiting four million years to feel the sea breeze again, sense sandpipers returning from Africa. But all of this might be a shaggy-dog story or Ray's own slippage of fact and fantasy. The field mice are stirring.

Scientists use the thigh
bone to map a sequence of
DNA proteins.
Who knew collagen could last
longer than four million years?

Puppet Speak

I hang in the window of the toy shop in East Runton. My head lolls to one side. I watch flocks of mothers, buggies stuffed with kids. Older siblings peer at me through the dirty window. The grubbier boys stare, furtive smiles, fingering change in their pockets. I imagine them unpicking my stitches under the cover of darkness and duvets. My companions are suspended from the ceiling: two swinging on long springs. If a customer pulls at their ankles, they shoot up and down in a wild dance, limbs flapping like corvids on the wing. *A murder of crows.* When you're left hanging in a window all day, your thoughts darken.

The world-famous *Fresh-
water Bed* is exposed when
Norfolk weather is wild.

The back of our shop houses a miniature theatre where children can choose sets, puppets and dream up shows. There are rats beneath the floorboards, but Lucinda doesn't mention them, hoping they will slip away from noisy, sticky-fingered kids. A girl called Daisy brings in a mammoth made of chicken-wire, PVA and tissue paper. I can see Lucinda is impressed.

Between *Fresh Water
Forest Bed* and chalk, *Wroxham
Crag* also yields fish
and mammal remains, and any-
thing from deer to whale fossils.

Daisy's allowed to root around the wicker drawers where our components are stored: wooden heads in one basket, kapok stuffed bodies in another, noses and eyes jostled together and small hats, made of red and blue matted felt. These bits and bobs of puppet-life wait patiently in the dark. Like parts of speech or half-forgotten phrases. We all want the chance to be stitched together and take to the stage.

Not I

These spoon-shaped parts of us are singing. A chorus of frogs, perhaps, or little open mouths. I am struggling to recall the play where the mouth performs. At first, I think Brecht and then think Beckett.

I knew that woman in Ireland, he said, I knew who she was – not 'she' specifically, one single woman, but there were so many of those old crones, stumbling down the lanes, in the ditches, besides the hedgerows.

I'm stumbling down the hill from Old Town. I sight half a rainbow and no pot of gold. My face is buffeted by the north wind and it begins to hail, stinging my cheeks. My mouth's full of nettles. Awake now. For fuck's sake, I'm wide awake and kicking the start of the year into the long grass where it belongs. Crone is a strong word but I will take it on the chin – happy to be witch-like; valued for wisdom, compassion, experience. I'm expecting nothing but the warmth of a mug of builder's tea and the stone walls of my cottage in its muddy field.

Dancing Slippers

Our words went out in their nightclothes when the moon was up. They were nimble and giddy, wore dancing slippers made of silk and left us for hours. We couldn't speak. We were mute, dumb creatures waiting for the words to finish their shenanigans. Some words hung back and our sentences had pauses, more gaps than before. We gestured and signed and made do with the words we had. Their slippers were threadbare; the dancing continued throughout that long, sweltering summer.

The temperature soared to new heights. We tried to sleep by putting sheets in the freezer. The words looked back at the human beings and pitied us all as the ground dried up.

The Shut Drawer

Since the meltdown, I've lived under a blanket of felt and groggy mornings. Withdrawal from years of anti-depressants is a wooden roller coaster. I picture the doctor, prescribing mirtazapine like candy, leaning forward and patting my knee. My body is pink light shimmering with love, then a permanent X-ray, bones glowing and skin transparent. Sleep, when it comes, is erratic with lucid dreams. One night, a would-be lover is powering up the M1 in a DeLorean. Typical, I think, passionate and completely impractical. Where does one buy a spare door for such a vehicle these days?

    I dream of a thief breaking in through the basement, playing the piano badly. But the family's Zender piano was long gone. Another night, outlying fields are being crop-sprayed with DDT. Night is *not for sleeping. It is for loosening the parts of yourself you forget in the daytime. It is for remembering that you are a force that goes on in spite of yourself.*

    The crop-plane swoops low, droning overhead. I am an egg with a shell so thin I could crack open under the kindest touch. Compassion is a closed drawer to me now.

The Roost

We picture all the departed ones as egrets on the river Aire. We stumble across them behind a Lidl supermarket and Vue Cinema, on a calm stretch of water surrounded by sycamore. There's a sanctuary here in the forgotten backwaters of the city. And warmth. The snowy birds wait together as the evening fades. A fisherman disturbs them and they rise up like ghosts, circling the weir. We glimpse Mother flying low over the water. She's no longer careworn and sepia in colour. Her elegant legs are outstretched as she glides on white, tapering wings.

Selected Poetry Titles Published by SurVision Books

Contemporary Tangential Surrealist Poetry: An Anthology
Edited by Tony Kitt
ISBN 978-1-912963-44-7

Invasion: An Anthology of Ukrainian Poetry about the War
Edited by Tony Kitt
ISBN 978-1-912963-32-4

Helen Ivory. *Maps of the Abandoned City*
(New Poetics: England)
ISBN 978-1-912963-04-1

Tony Kitt. *The Magic Phlute*
(New Poetics: Ireland)
ISBN 978-1-912963-08-9

Tony Bailie. *Mountain Under Heaven*
(Winner of James Tate Poetry Prize 2019)
ISBN 978-1-912963-09-6

Alison Dunhill. *As Pure as Coal Dust*
(Winner of James Tate Poetry Prize 2020)
ISBN 978-1-912963-23-2

Aoife Mannix. *Alice under the Knife*
(Winner of James Tate Poetry Prize 2020)
ISBN 978-1-912963-26-3

Becki Hawkes. *The Naming of Wings*
(Winner of James Tate Poetry Prize 2021)
ISBN 978-1-912963-34-8

Order our books from http://survisionmagazine.com

www.ingramcontent.com/pod-product-compliance
Lightning Source LLC
Chambersburg PA
CBHW071314060426
42444CB00035B/2651